Water Awareness Newborns
Part of the Water Awareness Series

by AlyT and Born To Swim

Formatting: Max Kuchin
Illustrator: Emets Anna Alekseevna
First printing: November, 2021

www.BornToSwim.com.au
SwimMechanics@yahoo.com
Other books in our Water Awareness Series include:
Water Awareness Newborns
Water Awareness Babies
Water Awareness Toddlers

'...You knitted me together
in my mother's womb.
I praise You,
for I am fearfully
and wonderfully made;

Psalm 139:13-14

Safety First

Supervise

Newborns (and young children) require strict and constant supervision in and around water AT ALL TIMES. It is important, before bathing or commencing an aquatic lesson, you turn off & tune out all distractions and prepare the workspace. Be very conscious of how much water baby ingests during their lesson and baths and NEVER LEAVE infants (or young children) unattended around water. Regardless of age and ability, no child or person is drown proof.

Submersions

We do not encourage submersion of infants before the age of 6 months. An infant's sucking reflex makes it difficult for babies at this age to resist taking in water. Excessive ingesting of water can cause water intoxication and poses a very serious health risk. Rushing to submerge a baby who has not learnt breath control can frighten baby resulting in an aversion to water and an increased occurrence of hyponatremia (excessive water ingesting). For more information search: Hyponatremia.

Slipping Hazards

Shower recesses, bathtubs and bathrooms contain slippery surfaces and tripping hazards. At the conclusion of the lesson, we advise having another person available to assist taking the slippery baby out of the bath or shower for you, if you have no one to assist you, think ahead by having warm towels within arms reach and a pram or portable bassinette nearby to place baby in when you have finished the lesson.

Stay Warm

The optimal water temperature for bathing and teaching babies is 30C (86F). Check the water temperature and adjust it accordingly before placing baby into a bath or shower that is too hot or too cold. Lesson duration times should not exceed 30mins, always aim to finish the lesson before baby shows signs of hunger, tiredness or becomes unsettled. Very young infants do not shiver and can become cold quickly, they should be removed from the water if they display signs of body heat loss.

Support your baby

Newborn Infants have minimal head control, their heads should be properly supported to prevent swallowing of excessive amounts of water and neck injuries. Please read our guide to proper baby holds in the next section.

Before we begin...

Hello Buoys & Gulls

At Born to Swim we have designed a series of 'Water Awareness' books to assist parents and carers in introducing infants and babies to water as a set of first steps on their aquatic journey. We believe creating a positive, safe association with water in the early years plays an important role in shaping a keenness and responsiveness to swimming later in life.

Our book offers easy to follow instructions and illustrations using a range of suitable, safe and enjoyable aquatic activities to be undertaken two to three times a week as a simple, repetitive water awareness routine. Your mood and disposition will influence how much you both enjoy your lesson and time together so arrange to conduct your bath time lessons at a time of day suitable to you and bub.

The purpose of this book is to act as a guide only for parents (of newborn infants - 6 month old) on how to familiarise baby with water and to prepare them for future aquatic programs. We do not recommend introducing infants to public pools until after 6 months of age to start their formal aquatic swim lessons. Water hygiene, loud noises and the effects of pool water chemicals can have a negative effect on baby, whereas at home instruction gives a more personable and bonding experience to baby in fresh, clean water.

Yours swimmingly,
Aly T

Ps. Remember to use a gentle voice (cooing, songs, verbal cues and laughter), sustained eye contact and loads of encouraging facial expressions during baby's lessons and they'll soon learn to love and respect the water.

Aquatic Holds for Infants

Learning how to hold baby in the water will assist baby to feel safe and secure. They must feel balanced and supported in the water at all times to maximise enjoyment.

Heart2Heart

Heart to Heart or Chest to Chest Hold gives postural support to newborn infants. It is a very comforting hold, giving baby maximum skin to skin contact and warmth. This hold is perfect for use in showers if you do not have access to a bathtub or baby bath. It is also used for practical purposes such as climbing out of showers and baths. One hand is protectively placed around baby's back to support their heads whilst the other is placed under baby's bottom to support baby's weight.

Lap Hold

The Lap Hold has the parent or carer sitting in shallow warm water with legs extended out front. Baby is laid back and supported on the parent's upper thighs. The parent can look over the baby with baby facing away from the parent OR maintain eye contact by having baby facing parent. Bending the knees of the parent or carer can assist in supporting baby when they are sitting upright.

Prone Float Hold

The Prone Float Hold is ideal for young babies with little neck control. Your arms are extended out front with hands supporting baby under their chest. The thumbs support baby's chin to keep their mouth and nose clear of the water whilst maintaining optimal eye contact.

Hand support under the head

When back floating baby's head and neck are supported by your hand and their upper back supported by your forearm. Baby's arms and legs can move freely to kick and splash or to float quietly.

Conditioning

The conditioning process, using tactile and verbal cues, teaches baby to hold their breath on command to help prevent ingestion or inhalation of water and to prepare baby for submersions when they commence a learn to swim program after 6 months of age.

During the first few weeks, to condition baby and to stimulate their reflex to hold their breath, we gently sprinkle water on baby's head and face using our hands, followed by gently wiping our wet fingertips down baby's face to soothe and reassure them.

BORNTOSWIM.COM.AU

EmetsAnn

Conditioning

Over the following weeks, as baby progresses, we condition baby by pouring small cups of water over their faces. To begin, sit baby upright and look into their eyes, support the back of their neck with your hand and forearm. Before wetting baby we say their 'name' to get their attention, 'ready' to prepare them and on 'go', using our free hand either gently sprinkle water on baby's face or pour a small cup of water smoothly over the front of their face. Baby will stiffen when the water or your fingertips wipe water down their face, this reflex is normal. Over time, with consistent, regular practice baby will begin to understand what to expect.

Aim for 4-5 conditioning pours during the lesson.

Back Float

Back floating teaches baby to relax and float on their back. Floating is the basis for learn to swim and an essential survival skill when in water.

Holding baby lightly but firmly on their back in the water enables baby to feel their buoyancy. Laying still they will enjoy the peacefulness of the water, swishing baby gently from side to side through the water on their back will allow them to feel the sensation of the moving water.

Back Float

To back float, lay baby on their back on your outstretched arm with their ears under the water, maintain eye contact as you support baby gently with your forearm cradling their head in your hand to support their necks.

For additional sensory stimulation, talk and coo as you pour a small cup of water over their body, avoiding their face, and allow baby to freely kick and splash as they explore the water.

Front Float

Front floats teach baby how to float in the prone position on their tummy, like back floats they are also an essential to the learn to swim journey.

Softly hold baby in the water on their belly, let the water support baby's body as you maintain eye contact and reassure them verbally with your voice and visually with your facial expressions. Swishing baby slowly from side to side will allow them to feel their buoyancy and the sensation of the water holding them. As baby progresses and becomes more comfortable in the water, encourage spontaneous kicking and random arm movements as they explore their movements in water.

To front float, lay baby flat in the water on their stomach with your arms extended and wrists together to form a 'v' under their chin. Fingers are splayed around baby's chest, and thumbs are placed under baby's chin to ensure their mouth and nose are kept clear of the water.

Assisted Kicking

Assisted coordinated kicking teaches baby how to move the water with their legs and feet.

At this stage of life, babies are too small to propel themselves through the water and their movements are involuntary. Moving baby's legs and feet using a coordinated kick will help create a muscle memory of the flutter kick and butterfly kick which they will learn later on in their swimming journey.

Lay baby on your forearms facing away from you, eye contact is maintained by looking over the top of baby. Use the verbal cue 'kick, kick, kick' as you gently grasp baby's legs from under the water, putting your thumbs over their knees to initiate a gentle splashing kick by baby. Flutter kick is simulated kicking one foot up and down at a time, to simulate butterfly kick simply kick both feet in the water together.

Using your hands to kick baby's legs should act as a guiding support only and should not involve any forced movements.

Grips

A strong grip is an essential water safety skill for baby. Later in their swimming journey baby will use their grip to hold onto their parent or carer in the water, grasp the side of the pool and pull themselves out of the water.

To practice strengthening baby's grip, sit baby upright in your lap with their back supported by your bent knees. Allow baby to grasp your thumbs and gently lift them towards you, being careful not to let their grip slip or to lift them too high.

Grip strengthening can also be practised during nappy changes and on other soft surfaces throughout the day, not just at bath time.

BACK

ROLL

BORNTOSWIM.COM.AU

FRONT

Rotation

Horizontal rotation will play an important role in baby's swimming journey as they get older and is an important lead-up to learning how to roll smoothly from their front to their back and from their back onto their front by themselves in water.

At this young age, baby will need your help and support to roll over safely in the water.

Rotating from Front-to-Back
To roll baby from their front onto their back, start by holding baby on their front using the prone float hold. Place one hand splayed firmly on baby's back, the other hand cradles their chin to keep baby's face out of the water as you roll them slowly onto their back.

Rotating from Back-to-Front
Have baby floating on their back, with their feet pointing away from you. Your hands support baby by holding them at their shoulders with fingers under their upper back. To initiate the roll, place one hand on their chest whilst the other hand supports baby's head, neck and upper back. Slowly roll baby onto their chest. Adjust your hands to provide support under baby's chin and to keep their nose and mouth clear from the water.

That's a wrap...

Wriggling, kicking and splashing in the water acts as a gentle exercise for baby and can stimulate baby's appetite, have a relaxing effect on baby, and enhance their sleep. Always end baby's lesson on a happy note before they become too tired, cold or hungry.

Remember to dry baby thoroughly before reclothing them. We suggest cradling your dry baby on their side for a short while after their lesson to ensure excess water drains from their ears before putting them down for their sleep.

And before you relax please ensure all bath tubs and baby baths are immediately emptied of water after each lesson.

...but that's just the beginning!

At 6 months, with lots of practice and praise, baby will be
ready to move onto the next stage of water awareness.
Look out for our Water Awareness — Babies
and
Water Awareness — Toddlers to continue their aquatic
journey.